In Our Own Words

Teen Art and Writing

Edited by Erin Ash Sullivan
and Keren Taylor

STECK-VAUGHN

Ⓖ Harcourt Supplemental Publishers

www.steck-vaughn.com

Photography: Cover, p.i ©Sam Dudgeon; p.7 ©John Curry; p.11 ©John Curry; p.12 ©John Curry; p.40 ©John Curry.

Additional photography by Artville, Corbis Royalty Free, and Bill Smith Studio Collection.

Art: Cover, p.i Joan Cunningham; p.iv Matthew Gilli; p.2 Dan Van Blarcom; p.4 Katelyn Hyman; p.7 Hailey Coonrad; p.11 Lori Drewes; p.12 Ryan Foy; p.17 Chris Scala; p.18 Alexandra Breitenbach; p.22 Hangyeol Ryu; p.26 Ariel Davis; p.31 Matthew Gilli; p.34 Scott Pagano; p.37 Ariel Davis; p.40 Nathan Karl.

ISBN 0-7398-7536-1

Power Up! Building Reading Strength is a trademark of Steck-Vaughn.

Printed in China.

1 2 3 4 5 6 7 8 9 M 07 06 05 04 03

Contents

Introduction

All the poems and short stories in this book were written by teens. All the art was created by teens, too.

Some of the pieces are about things that are important to the writer or artist: friends, family, hobbies, sad times, and happy times. Some of the works are about things that happened in real life. Other works come straight from the writer's or artist's imagination. All of these teens have something important to say about what it feels like to be them.

Who Are the Writers and Artists?

The teen writers and artists in this book are between 13 and 18 years old. They are all quite different from one another.

Some of the teens have lived in the United States their whole lives. Others have emigrated from another country to the United States. Some are confident writers and artists, while others are just starting.

Even though they're different in many ways, they all have something in common. They've found that writing or creating art is a great way to share their thoughts and ideas.

Dan Van Blarcom, 16

How Did the Writers Do It?

All of the teen writers in this book started by writing a first draft to get their ideas down on paper. They worked with adults and other teen writers to make their piece better. Then the writers wrote more drafts.

All of the writers learned how important it was to read their piece to others. This helped them decide what sounded good and what needed to change. The writers also learned that even when writing was scary and difficult, it felt good to put their thoughts into words. They learned that the more they wrote, the better they got.

Art and Ideas

Some people feel more comfortable sharing their ideas through pictures. The teen artists in this book used lines, colors, and shadows to show their thoughts and feelings.

Maybe this book will inspire you to write, draw, or paint something of your own!

Chapter 1

The Real Me

"Who is the real me?" This is a hard question that many teens think about often. Some teens try to figure out who they are by changing how they look on the outside.

Teens also take the time to think about who they are inside, though. Often they compare themselves with others. They wonder how to please their friends, their families, and most of all, themselves. They think about what it takes to be happy and responsible. They think about what it means to grow up.

The teen writers in this chapter have all asked, "Who am I?" They have come up with very different answers.

◀ Katelyn Hyman, 17

In this poem, Kyla Winston compares herself to everything from a rain puddle to a kind of tree called a willow.

I Am Me

I am me . . .
tasty like a leaf made of tea,
smooth like the weeds of the sea.
I am me . . .
shallow like rain puddles,
as deep as the Nile,
dry like the desert sand, running for miles.
I am me . . .
a sniff of the morning air,
something you've never heard of.
Yet I'm a part of you,
the sugar in your coffee, the milk in your tea,
I am once more that person called ME . . .
I'm sticky and icky, clean and quiet,
I am me . . .
weeping like a willow, soft as a pillow.
I AM ME!

—Kyla Winston, 15

What's in a name? For Olivia Linares, it's everything from what she wears to the date she was born. In this piece she tells how her names stand for different parts of who she is.

Oli

My name is Olivia Magdalena Linares. My dad gave me this name because my grandma has it. In Spanish, my name means "peaceful." In school, my friends sometimes call me Tweety because I wear yellow. Sometimes they call me Pinky because I wear pink. At home, they call me Oli. In school, my friends call me Olive, Olivi, and 27, because it is the date of my birthday.

—Olivia Linares, 15

Hailey Coonrad, 15

How do you feel when people judge you? How do you feel when you judge yourself? Stephanie Passman writes about an unhappy friend who worries about what other people think of him.

Judged by Success

Being judged by success is something
that Scrooge in *A Christmas Carol*
knows about.
Woody makes me think of him
because he looks angry.
He has bags under his eyes
as if he stays up all night worrying.
He wishes he wasn't as sad as he is
and that he would have one friend
because he's lonely,
but he can't.
He wouldn't know how
to trust anybody.

—Stephanie Passman, 15

Sometimes we might feel that we must show different sides of ourselves when we're with different people. Oscar Morales writes about how happy he feels with his best friend, no matter what side he shows.

Two Sides of Me

I have two sides.
I have a good side and a bad side.
I am someone
with a lot of different feelings.
The person who evens me out
is my best friend.
Everyone needs something
to get through the day.
For some people, it's music.
For others, it's sports.
For me, it's my best friend.
Both sides of me are happy
when I'm with her.

—Oscar Morales, 17

Meeting someone from a different culture can make you think differently about yourself. In this story, Sheena Apilado writes about how a pair of brown eyes changed the way that she saw herself.

Pretty Brown Eyes

I never liked sleeveless shirts. I always thought, *I don't like my arms*. Once, my family was on a trip to the Philippines when I saw the prettiest set of eyes. The woman passing by me had the most lovely pair of brown eyes I'd ever seen. I had never really looked closely at eyes before, so I wondered what made hers so special.

Then I saw that her eyes were the only part of her body that wasn't covered. She was an Arab woman traveling with her husband. I later learned that some women of certain cultures are not allowed to show their arms or legs. Everything has to be covered. I don't see why some women are not even allowed to show their elbows. Even this woman's face was hidden behind that pretty cloth, except those brown eyes.

After that day, I fell in love with every piece of clothing I owned, even the sleeveless shirts.

—Sheena Apilado, 17

Lori Drewes, 14

Chapter 2

Express Yourself

When you wake up in the morning, what do you look forward to? What do you live for? Everybody has something that he or she loves to do. It might be a sport, such as football or baseball. It might be something creative, like acting, writing, or painting. It might even be something as simple as talking with a friend.

Why are our hobbies so important? They let us have fun. They make us feel like experts. Most of all, they give us a chance to express ourselves!

The stories and poems in this chapter show how some teens express themselves. How do you express yourself?

◀ Ryan Foy, 18

In this poem, Simon Cowart writes about the joy that he finds in making his own choices.

The Coin

I flip the coin.
I go where I want,
do what I want,
see what I want,
taste what I want,
feel what I want,
know what I want.
The world belongs to me.

—Simon Cowart, 15

Jenna Ruth's poem explains how it feels when someone gives up her own thoughts and goes along with the mainstream.

Left Behind

No action without a motive,
no motive without a mind,
no mind without a heart—
this dream, she left behind.

She traveled over mountains,
she traveled over lakes.
Nature gave her freedom.
She never thought she'd make mistakes.

Foolish but thoughtful, this woman
was once so happily free.
Now drowning in the mainstream,
how sad a woman is she.

—Jenna Ruth, 14

For some teens, there is nothing better than performing in a show for other people. Jackie Bressack writes about what it feels like to be on stage and hear the applause.

On Stage

Your heart is beating hard. Your stomach seems to drop all the way to your feet. You get a sudden rush to the top of your head. It's show time! I express myself through acting. When I'm on a stage in front of an audience, it feels like I'm running the show. Nobody can tell me my acting is too much or too little. I can take a chance, take the part over the top, and make it my own.

I was just in *Peter Pan*, where I got to play Captain Hook. It was great! Near the end of the play, the boy playing Peter pretended to push me off the stage. This was my moment. I leaned back and waved my arms. I was supposed to fall off the stage, but I didn't.

I stood there just to be funny. I looked as though I was about to fall, and the audience started to laugh. I kept pretending to fall, and they kept laughing. Finally, when the music stopped, I jumped. The applause was huge.

This is why I want to be on stage. You can be creative. You can make the audience feel for your character.

—Jackie Bressack, 13

Chris Scala, 15

Chapter 3

Roadblocks

Every teen is faced with roadblocks in life. A roadblock could be the death of a loved one or losing a friend. It could be moving far away and having to leave home forever. Maybe you missed the winning kick in a big football game and feel as though you let down the team.

The teen writers in this chapter have all suffered through different problems. They were strong enough to get past their roadblocks and move on with their lives. How do you solve problems and get through the hard times?

◀ Alexandra Breitenbach, 18

In history class, Alma Castrejon learned that Spanish explorers came to Mexico and Central America and took the land for themselves. In 1521 the explorers wiped out the city of Tenochtitlán and built Mexico City on top of the ruins. What Alma learned inspired her to write this poem about her Hispanic roots.

I Am From

I am from Tenochtitlán
where much blood was spilled.
I am from a land of mighty warriors
who fought to give me freedom.
I am from a place that Hernán Cortés
wiped from the face of the earth.
I am from a place
where freedom no longer exists.

I am from a place where we
remember the dead.
I am from a place
of real heroes like Benito Juárez,
Comandante Marcos, and
Emiliano Zapata.

I am from a world of broken dreams.
I am from a world that
gets me ready to face the future.

I am from somewhere that
is giving me a chance.
I am from a place where
a great future waits for me—
if I follow that path.
I am from Tenochtitlán.
I am from a land of
mighty warriors.

—Alma Castrejon, 17

Being a team leader can be great, but it can be hard when your team loses. In this piece, Jake Morayniss writes about the pressure of being the person in charge.

Hangyeol Ryu, 18

The Playoffs

I was the starting quarterback this year on the football team. Our coach said that it was my job to lead the team. If the team made a mistake, it would be my fault because I was in charge. I wasn't used to being a leader, but I was ready to try.

We went to the playoffs with a 7–4 record. We went into our first playoff game feeling good. The other team had lost to us once before, 26–0.

At halftime, we were winning 26–6. Then one of our best players got kicked out of the game for being a bad sport. We lost our lead. We lost the game by two points.

I felt responsible for losing the game because I was the quarterback. However, I had to get over it and move on. This football season made me a stronger person. It taught me how to deal with pressure. It made me more confident. It also taught me how to be a leader, even during the hard times.

—Jake Morayniss, 14

When Fawwad Memon's family emigrated from Pakistan to the United States, they left many friends and relatives behind. Fawwad's poem is about the sadness he feels for the people he misses.

Say Goodbye

I just think and think
how much I miss my friends.
I wish I could see them again.
I won't forget those memories
when we said goodbye.
I remember when everyone
was crying.
I hope I see all of them again
sometime in my life.

—Fawwad Memon, 15

Claudia Torres tells how she exists and stays strong in a world filled with sadness.

I Am Standing Strong

I can't stand to watch
brothers and sisters dying,
mothers and fathers crying
in this city where I have spilled so many tears,
and yet . . .
Among those dying young
and the old ones who suffer so,
I stand and grow.
I am standing strong and tall,
even though others fall.
I am standing
through the strongest storms,
the most burning suns,
the blackest rains.
I keep my eye on tomorrow,
my feet on a clear path.
Hold my hand.
I am standing strong and tall.

—Claudia Torres, 17

Chapter 4

Close Ties

One of the most important things in our lives is how we deal with other people. We learn through our relationships with friends and family. They help us change and grow.

Who has helped you in your life? Which person means the most to you? Maybe it's a parent. Maybe it's another relative, like an aunt or a grandfather. Maybe it's a best friend.

No matter who the person is, everyone has a close relationship with someone. Sometimes the relationship goes smoothly, and sometimes it doesn't. The writers in this chapter tell about some of their relationships.

Brothers and sisters can be the worst of enemies and the best of friends. Jeffrey Blum's story is about his relationship with his brother.

Two of a Kind

My brother Greg is four years older than I am. We have had some good times and some bad times. When I was little, he was nice, but he also loved to bother me.

Once, I got a toy for my birthday. Greg said that I couldn't play with it because he had to test it. He said he had to make sure that it was okay. Well, that made sense to me because I was only a little child. I didn't know what was going on.

After a while, I asked him if I could have the toy back. He said, "You'll have to give me some money if you want to play with your toy." I gave him some money, and he finally let me play with my toy. I later got my money back, but this kind of thing really got to me.

Sometimes I bothered Greg instead. A while ago, I was watching a video from when I was about two years old. On the video, I was playing with my blanket, and my brother took it from me. He put it over his head and spun in circles. I looked at him and charged. He fell over. I got my blanket back and I was happy.

The other day, my dad told me a story about when Greg and I were little. Greg was playing with his toys. I was throwing blocks at him. He started crying. My dad came in and asked, "What's happening?" Greg said, "Jeff is throwing blocks at me!" My dad did not get mad at me, though. Instead he said, "Well, then, move! Don't just sit there!"

These days, my brother Greg and I are pretty close. That's hard to believe, after all we've been through together.

—Jeffrey Blum, 14

Mara Bochenek's poem is about the path of a teardrop.

Teardrop

The teardrop came down on the window
and rolled onto my cheek.
Then it fell into my hand,
where I gave it to my dad,
who gave it to my mom.
My mom gave it to my sister,
and she put it back on the window.
It rolled off onto the ground,
where it went to a friend in China.
She gave that very same teardrop
to her mom and dad.
She put it back on the window
and it came back to me
to keep in a jar forever and ever.
Now my jar is full of teardrops
from a friend in China.

—Mara Bochenek, 15

Matthew Gilli, 17 ▶

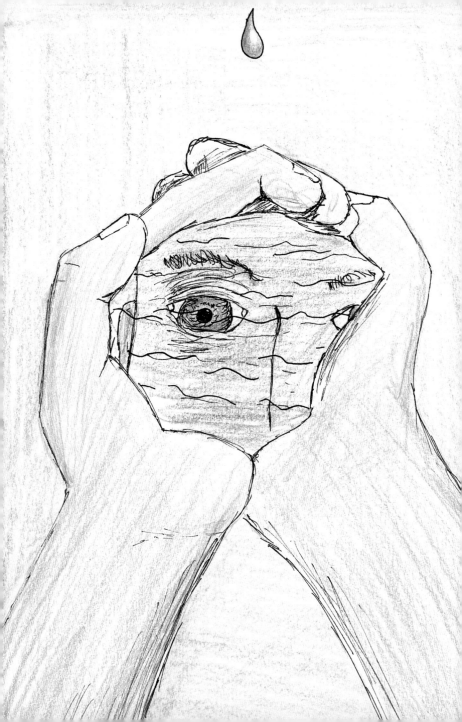

In this story, Amanda Gottesman writes about how her godmother changed her life.

A Kind Heart

I knew a woman who was brave, smart, and full of love. That woman was my godmother, Linda, and she died last year after getting sick. She inspired me to live my dreams and to have a kind heart.

I remember the little things we did together. When I slept over at Linda's house, we had special dinners and baked cookies. I often felt better talking to her about my life than to my mother. Linda was a relative, but she was also a friend.

It was hard to watch Linda's sickness take over. For so many years, she had helped me with my homework, told me stories, and packed my lunches. She had been a second mother to me.

Although Linda is no longer alive, I still learn from her. I want to leave the world a better place, just as Linda did.

—Amanda Gottesman, 14

This next piece is a set of song lyrics. As you read these lyrics, think about how they would sound if they were set to music. Angela Martinez wrote this song for a close friend.

Wave

A silent wave rushes through me.
A soft wind tickles me with its fingertips.
I walk along the warm, wide beach
and grab a shooting star
from the deep blue sky.
The moon talks to me with purple words.
I sing to the sky,
and tiny stars sing along.
Tiny stars sing along.

Look at me with your honey cat eyes.
Take me somewhere fresh.
I'll sing my life to you.
We can dance into our warm future,
dance into our warm future.

—Angela Martinez, 15

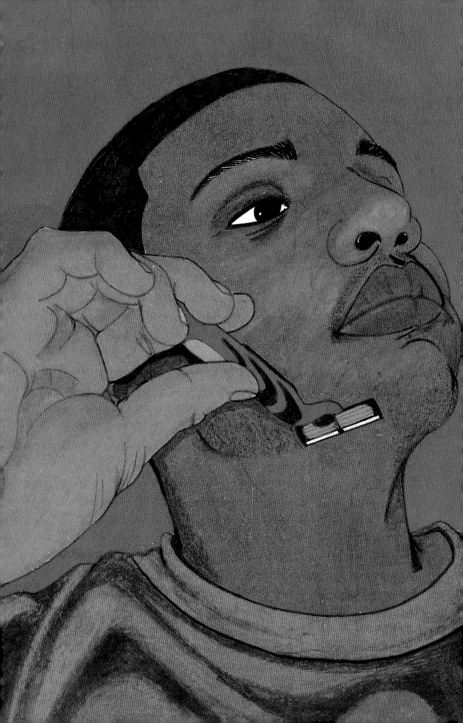

Chapter 5

Fast Forward

Does the future seem far away? Try to imagine yourself in ten or twenty years. What are your hopes and dreams? Where will you be? What will you be?

The teen writers in this chapter also think about the future. Their pieces show their wishes and fears about growing up.

Think about your own hopes and dreams. Are you on the right path? Put your own wishes and fears into words or art. This will help you understand where you are now and where you might be heading.

As we move on in life, we say goodbye to the past. In this story, Jennifer Gottesfeld shares memories of when she was younger.

Here's to Yesterday

Mommy and Daddy fought the monsters under my bed. They read me to sleep with *Good Night, Moon*. My biggest problem was when the scoop of ice cream dropped from my cone after just one lick. I cried because it seemed like the end of the world.

I was told not to bite my nails, not to eat the sand, not to talk back to the teacher. My eyes were brighter then. Around each corner was a new mountain waiting to be climbed. I dressed up in my ballet costume and danced around my living room to *Sleeping Beauty*. I could fit both my feet into one of Mommy's high-heel shoes.

There was a time when I would scream and cry when I had to leave my friend's house. I thought that tomorrow would be too long to wait until I could see her again.

Somewhere, lost between science and math, I forgot to look up at the moon. I forgot to pretend that I could fly, like I did when I was so much younger.

I forgot that there was a yesterday, because I was so wrapped up in worrying about tomorrow.

—Jennifer Gottesfeld, 16

Ariel Davis, 18

In his future, Clifford Bell wants to rhyme and move to his own beat. In this poem he writes about his dream.

....

Little Clifford Bell

My name is Clifford Bell.
I like to rap.
In the future
I am going to be a DJ.
When I feel an idea,
I throw it out
so all the world can hear me.
I can rap.
I can put something down on paper.
I can tell you about myself in rhyme.
Music calms me down.
I like to be happy all the time.
I make more friends
when I am happy.
Hear my words flow.
I am the DJ called
"Little Clifford Bell."

—Clifford Bell, 15

In nature, snakes shed their skin as they grow older. Some types of crabs leave their shells behind as they get bigger. What do you leave behind as you grow up? In this poem, Maria Monroy compares her experiences growing up to the life of a crab.

Moving to a New Self

Deep in the sea,
the water is as cold
as winter.
In the water,
a crab
moves to another self
because the crab has grown bigger
and has to move to a bigger self.
It leaves the old self
so another crab
can move to the one
the bigger crab left behind.

—Maria Monroy, 13

Nathan Karl, 17

Glossary

applause (uh PLAWZ) *noun* Applause is the clapping of people's hands after a good show.

chapter (CHAP tuhr) *noun* A chapter is a part of a book.

compare (kuhm PEHR) *verb* To compare things means to look at how they are the same or different.

confident (KAHN fuh duhnt) *adjective* Confident means certain or sure.

creative (kree AYT ihv) *adjective* Creative means having to do with a good imagination or using new ideas.

culture (KUHL chuhr) *noun* Culture is the ideas and ways of life of a group of people.

date (DAYT) *noun* A date is a particular day of a month or year.

DJ (DEE jay) *noun* A DJ is someone who works at a radio station or plays recorded songs for other people.

draft (DRAFT) *noun* A draft is a rough copy of a piece of writing.

dying (DY ihng) *adjective* Dying means having one's life come to an end.

emigrated (EHM ih grayt ihd) *verb* Emigrated means left one's country to live in another country.

exists (ehg ZIHSTS) *verb* Exists means is alive or real.

express (ehk SPREHS) *verb* To express means to show or put into words.

godmother (GAHD muhth uhr) *noun* A godmother is a close family friend who helps raise a child.

inspire (ihn SPYR) *verb* To inspire means to make other people want to do something.

lyrics (LIHR ihks) *noun* Lyrics are words to songs.

mainstream (MAYN streem) *noun* The mainstream is the way most people act or think.

motive (MOHT ihv) *noun* A motive is a reason for doing something.

playoffs (PLAY awfs) *noun* Playoffs are games where teams play against each other to choose a winner.

pressure (PREHSH uhr) *noun* Pressure is the feeling that you must do something.

quarterback (KWAHRT uhr bak) *noun* A quarterback is the player who calls the plays and passes the ball on a football team.

rap (RAP) *verb* To rap means to perform a kind of popular music in which words are spoken along with a beat.

relationships (rih LAY shuhn shihps) *noun* Relationships are the close ties people have with others.

relatives (REHL uh tihvz) *noun* Relatives are members of the same family.

responsible (rih SPAHN suh buhl) *adjective* Responsible means able to be trusted or being the cause of something.

rhyme (RYM) *verb* To rhyme is to write or say a set of words ending with the same sound.

roadblocks (ROHD blahks) *noun* Roadblocks are things that stop you from moving forward.

sleeveless (SLEEV lihs) *adjective* Sleeveless means having no sleeves.

suffered (SUHF uhrd) *verb* Suffered means went through a tough time.

teardrop (TIHR drahp) *noun* A teardrop is a tear that falls from one's eye.

teens (TEENZ) *noun* Teens are people between 13 and 19 years of age.

video (VIHD ee oh) *noun* A video is a movie.

warriors (WAWR ee uhrz) *noun* Warriors are people who fight in battles.

willow (WIHL oh) *noun* A willow is a kind of tree with long, bending branches.